MW00814549

Awake Despite the Hour

Paul Mitchell lives in the Melbourne suburb of Yarraville. His first poetry collection, *Minorphysics* (IP 2003), won the 2003 IP Picks Award for best unpublished Australian poetry manuscript. He was runner-up in the 2005 Arts Queensland Val Vallis Award for Poetry and he has received numerous awards and commendations for his work.

He has performed at New York's Bowery Poetry Club, the Melbourne Writers' Festival, the Newcastle Young Writers Festival, Big West Festival, Montsalvat Festival of Poetry and Song, and has been a feature at numerous Melbourne poetry venues. He has also written and performed two dramatic monologues, 'Sleepless in Braybrook' (the Yarraville Festival) and 'Get the Word' (La Mama Theatre, Melbourne). His spoken word CD, *As if nothing is happening . . . and it is*, co-produced with Bill Buttler, was released in 2005.

Paul's debut short fiction collection, *Dodging the Bull,* was released by Wakefield Press in 2007. A journalist, copywriter and teacher, Paul recently completed a MA in Creative Arts (Creative Writing) at the University of Melbourne on the poetry of Kevin Hart. In 2006 he was awarded an Australia Council grant to work on his first novel.

Kevin,
Thanks for the
inspiration and guidance
your poems and essays
have offered me from afar.
peace [signature]

Also by Paul Mitchell

Poetry

Minorphysics, Interactive Press, 2003

Short Fiction

Dodging the Bull, Wakefield Press, 2007

Awake Despite the Hour

Paul Mitchell

Five Islands Press

© **Paul Mitchell 2007**

This book is copyright. Apart from any fair dealing for the purposes
of study and research, criticism, review, or as otherwise permitted
under the Copyright Act, no part may be reproduced by any process
without written permission.
Inquiries should be made to the publisher.

Published by Five Islands Press Pty Ltd,
PO Box 1015 Carlton 3053
03 8344 8713
email: rpretty@unimelb.edu.au

Cover photograph: 'Crystalline'
Bernadette Keys with Ming-Zhu Hii
Author photograph:
Sarah Parr

National Library of Australia
Cataloguing-in-Publications Entry
Mitchell, Paul, 1968–
Awake despite the hour
ISBN 978 0 7340 3694 9

1. Title.
A821.3

This project was assisted by the Commonwealth Government
through the Literature Board of the Australia Council,
the Federal Government's arts funding and advisory body.

Acknowledgements

Versions of poems in this collection have appeared in:

The Age, The Australian, Antipodes, Blast, Blue Dog, The Canberra Times, Going Down Swinging, Malleable Jangle, Meanjin, Muse Anthology, National Indigenous Times, Overland, Quadrant, Slope, Southerly, and *Space New Writing.* Thanks to all the editors.

'Moral Comfort' was runner-up in the 2005 Arts Queensland Val Vallis Award.

For support, encouragement and assistance, my heartfelt thanks to: alicia sometimes, Kevin Brophy, Kevin Hart, Bruno Lettieri, the Rotunda Writers Group (you too, Dawn!), Ron Pretty, Joel Dean, Jillian Pattinson and Nathan Curnow. A special thanks to the anthologist John Leonard for his painstaking work on this book.

Awake Despite the Hour

Contents

11   Stage Fright
12   Lyrics For at Least One Love Song
13   Contact
14   Daughter and Orange
15   Snaps
16   At the Gates
18   Because it is Only an Orange
19   The Soldier
20   The Bells Flying
     Scenes From a Marriage
     22   *Drained*
     23   *Midnight Faery*
     24   *The Rocks*
25   The Devices We Are Left To
26   Moral Comfort
27   A Series of Good Investments
29   Prayer
30   Bedroom Psalm
31   Screen Print Activist
33   Character Actor
34   Gone Wonderland
35   Eclipse
36   You Say You Want a Revolution, Well...
37   All the News
38   American Might
39   ID
39   He Will Become a Musician
41   Convincing Ground

42   Even the Elect

43   Refurbishment

44   Essay After Interest

45   Lining Up Time

46   White Fluffy Clouds, Angels Playing Harps

47   Ode to a Frying Christ

48   Sharing the Lion's Share

49   Angle

50   Demographic Manifesto

52   Insight

53   Father's Club

54   My Wheelie Bin's Big Day

55   Baggage

56   Faultlines

57   Better Late Than, etc.

58   Required

59   ID

61   Practice

62   Dear Kids

63   You're Lying Again

64   How Many Light Bulbs Does it Take?

65   The Bedroom Clock

66   The Persistent Myth

67   Love Song for St Simeon

68   Review

69   Aftermath

70   Awake, Despite the Hour

Blessed are those who carry for they shall be lifted
– Anna Kamienska

for Bruno Lettieri,
a champion of poetry

Stage Fright

Spotlight shows
the actor shuts his mouth
fire without a flame

A fortune is made by the lost
the hamlet rage is over
all the world is all the world

Stage boards torn up
through the glass of houses
when we begin we will begin

Lyrics For at Least One Love Song

After driving most of the day,
you give up trafficking in society
and decide there are better ways
to make a loving. Or at least
other angles from which to view
the corpse of your former life.
It hangs in every tree you pass,
never more glistening now its breath
has gone, mist for lost birds to fly through.

Car door ajar, you bend and listen
to the road, expecting a heartbeat.
There is a rattle, a train carriage
coming loose, then rejoining.
The engine, which might be your car's,
keeps on with methodical digging.
Down there no one asks questions
about punctuality or what is the reason
for driving away. And not for the first time
today, you know the meaning of life:
love is a long, slow allegation. You stare
down the tunnel it makes.

Contact

Did you get my email? No, where'd you send it? To your work address.
I'm not on that address. Are you on your home address? Yeah, but I didn't
get a message. I got your text. I didn't send a text. Yes you did. The one
about your message. What message? The one you left on my work phone.
Oh, but I left one later on your home phone. I didn't get that one. Have
you had your mobile on? Yeah. Did you leave a message on it? No, but I
sent you a text. I didn't get that text. Was it the one about your email? No,
that was the one about my phone message. Which one? The one on your
home phone. Oh, I only check my home messages from my work phone.
Can I leave a new message on your mobile? Yeah, but don't use my work
mobile. Can I text to that one? Yeah, text to it, but don't call, you can
call and text to my home mobile, but remember I sometimes turn it off.
Can I come to your home? Text me first to see if I'm there. Or email me.
Okay, I can do that from my phone when I get to the door. It's been good
talking to you. Great to catch up. Talk to you soon. Yeah, okay. Wait on .
. .What? I'll take a picture. Can I pxt it to you later? Yeah, but not to my
work mobile. I'll email it to your hotmail. Cool.

Daughter and Orange

a still life

Daughter, hand over the orange.
Your attempt to peel it
has pockmarked it, released fragrance,
but you cannot eat it. Yet

give it to me and there is hope
you may one day taste it.

Thank you. Now watch –
Some prefer a knife
and the way the rind coils.
I dig my thumb inside
and pull.

Look, here are the pieces.
Their shapes fit your mouth.
Go on. Try one.

You don't want to? Okay,
but you will
when you peel your own.

Snaps

I want the day to end where it ends
and the night to begin. That is,
I've had enough of the desert
and all the creatures in it. Laugh scorpion
but I threw your tail into the sky.

The moon. Taking up too much of the night.
The horizon is happy without you. And so am I.

I've got enough sand to fill. The hourglass
is broken at the oasis, the palms drooping.
When I find my photograph I'll call for my horse.
Don't drain the image. I've got enough sun.

Cactus. A thorny story. And my feet
bleeding from tiny bullet holes. The ants
crawl in and out, disguised.

This is the miracle of heat. An endless ephiphany.
The sunlight picking me up by the shoulders.

At the Gates

Kafka saw gate after gate, world not within world,
but world without beginning. Then the rebounding
of future gates in our faces. Yet I like to imagine,
dream or believe that all the gates have been unhinged.
Stacked upon each other in a paddock, the shape,
if viewed from a certain angle, might be called religious.
But faded gold on each gate's side is the only reminder
(even Kafka agreed) they once held back light.
In the midst of death we are in life. The evidence?
The valley of the shadow of life holding
a sunstreaked river of death. Each skull and femur
bobbing in the water is thread through or tied with a flower.
Black for the colour of, red for the colour of, life in death,
flowing from the river to the wounds of those on shore.
Can these wet skins live like a dry bone floats?
Back in the city today, the same faces.
Birds scattered as birds will.
I climbed the highest building, the view
took me in: *That's where you were born.*
There's the golf course where all the buildings
are made. A child waved from the great height,
his arm flapping like a door handle.
In a brave act, I walked around fully clothed
(even my utterances) and expected attention.
I stripped myself of that notion
but only as far as the bathtub could sail me.
I try not to confess it, but all the gates
(and their authors) could open for nothing.
A cruel taskmaster, Nothing, the one
who brought me out of silence then gave me words,
reminders of how much I want to escape.
Shhh, don't be afraid. Nothing is happening.

But I've come this far! If this is as far as I am . . .
How much further? What gate? Let me get out
of the car, plane, life and unlock it, it can't be
that difficult. Far from difficult. Far from anything
that's far, behind a galaxy or planet, far inside an atom.
I'm looking out and smiling for the camera,
there's always a camera, if not an eye,
at least a punctuation mark.
I will set my table, but no longer eat there.
I will gather up my breadsticks and be
somewhere out wherever floating is allowed,
wherever the locks of the river are opened,
whatever information the boat beneath my feet is leaking.

Because it is Only an Apple

she eats it in the garden, enjoys it.
The crowd cries out for more
but she takes one bite at a time.
Thank you, thank you, thank you,
she nods and no one notices she's naked
wearing singlet top and jeans.
No one asks who will come
to sweep away the core and pips,
soak the juice from off the grass.
Details like this are best left
to the scribes and those who
analyse what the scribes will say
(I didn't see anyone taking notes).

The Soldier

patrols your house in moonlight,
his shadow on your couch.
When was your house bombed?
It doesn't bother him
and neither does the darkness.
His General said,
You're at one with darkness.
He has no reason to doubt this,
no reason to be anything
but a soldier walking.

Beneath his feet your house creaks
and you wonder, will he open fire
on empty chairs? Your wounds
from love and hate and years
say *Yes, Yes, Yes,* and then,
as if confirmation were required,
his rifle butt thumps your floorboards.

Behind the one locked door,
secure upon a wall, hangs the photo
of the house before the bombs.
You know that soon he'll shoot the door,
kick it till his soles are bruised.
It won't open, but he'll walk away
convinced he'll break it down tomorrow.

The Bells Flying
for Felicity

The bells of the liturgy are flying
in from the ocean and over the town.
Pine trees stretch at the fence
then kick the clouds around;
the clouds, the bells, the liturgy.

Gulls wander the beach, wintered, chipless,
and you're there in your eagle coat,
swarmed in history, plagued
by opportunity, the bells
are in the church spire and the clocktower
and in that graveyard where they'll bury you
if you get the chance to live.

Pine needles over your skin
but you're not lying down
in the sun's blank stare, its usual
long, slow winter glance at you.
The bells of the liturgy pass through
the empty bluestone church, pews built
with ship's mahogany, treasure chests
for the blessed absent, their God
never more here now he's gone.

The wind's replaced, too, by chimes
hung from homes on clifftops,
the white-capped waves, neighbourhood watchers,
a flowing uniform, a liquid constabulary,
guarding telescopes that point away
from windows, toward TV screens.
Seagulls peck at the brick veneer:
Coastal Views for Sale – enquire within
the depths of our black eyeballs.

You're still there on the beach, your coat
is hung from a stick you've anchored in sand.
Scare, seagull, scare, but they don't, they stand
on the shoulder of your coat. You throw them
crusts from the bread you're eating,
but they fly past, straight for your loaf.
And the bells of the liturgy fly the beach,
short bomber raids, you raise your hands
in the air, but the air won't hold them.

Can you hear the bells of football training,
the *dump*, the *dump* of balls on boots,
the bells that fly from hand to hand?
Under single floodlight they shine,
they are shooting stars that explode
into the chests of men who believe
in only skin – the red leather, throbbing placentas,
it's the love of the game, the love of all things
that fly through the air, as long as they land again
in sure and calloused hands. The bells of the liturgy are,
you just have to look, shaped like skirts.

The lamp will be taken from the seven churches
of Smyrna and also of Portland. Yours is unplugged,
stored with your dog collar, your four-wheel-drive
is running, the boxes are packed, the congregation
is fully clothed and bathing under winter sun.
The bells of the liturgy flutter over your roof racks
then land, more baggage for the journey.

Scenes From a Marriage

Drained
after Off, *a sketch by Patricia Wade*

A shadow of your former self
before self mattered to you: white space
closed by curved horizons, holding
some emptiness. But you hold your own.

Your glance, permanently away
to where your life was, unaware
of what life's still drawing from you
in the shape of me. It's too late, I know,

to give you palette loads
of primary school colours.
You would fling them from your back
stay crouched, stay ready
to sprint into your background.

Midnight Faery

after a painting by Vanot Joan

I am not visible to you
so don't imagine a finger
pressed to my thin lips is anything
more than a feather on a branch.

Allow me my winged boots;
and where you can't see, I've landed:
a mound of leaves torn from trees
shaken by my magic. This smile

is not for you, nor the shimmer
from my pirouetting legs . . . But
keep watch – I'll lash you in a blink
and bring my gift of fear.

The Rocks

after Lake Eildon, *a painting by Duff Cecil*

Why does one boat upturn and another float,
one headland diminish and another enlarge?
Blame the wind, the moist air that's sticking plaster
on wounds that can't be seen. But the lake

is still now, smooth as ancient medicine.
The hills were once filled with nothing more
than what they're filled with now: memory,
bracken, the strangled truth of birdcalls,

the lying grass. Trees, of course, stand around,
watching: it's not in their nature to divulge.
The sun flexes in a mirror on the other side
of the atmosphere, the night taps on its watch

and sighs. The words *I can't* painted on the sky
in clouds that break up, then fight to reform. So many
stones on the shore now for a child to throw,
hard miracles to unravel across the water, then fall,

breaking silence, breaking vows of gratitude for earth,
sunlight and companionship. The two boats have found
their way to shore, one motionless, upturned,
the other rocking, buoyant. But both are empty,

despite sure hulls and steady timber. Tadpoles
were the only witnesses to their journeys; swimming
behind wooden fortresses that guarded them from
a lake that would not ripple, a storm that would not break.

The Devices We Are Left To

seem harmless enough, ticking in the garden shed
or tucked in the cupboard with the toaster. They each
have a name, but why speak them? They won't reply.
Known to wander at night, they gather beneath the passionfruit vine.
They take out inventories, tick off every second of our lives.
Our yearning for more time amazes them. They pull out menus
and order time to go. Some should be in boxes marked, Warning.
Others could sit neatly on a shelf with soft toys. They are like strangers
reading on park benches, looking up only when ignored. They come
in primary colours, but mix and mix until they are night sky in full cloud.
Their overheads are enormous, but free. Take one in your hands!
Feel how perfectly it fits. Press it – hard, but malleable. They have
their own power source. Sit back and enjoy. Hum along if you like.

Moral Comfort

After all this wandering what is there left
but more wandering? Several teeth in a jar
and an apparent loss of consciousness,
a fading of the curtain under pressure of light,
all the dancing has stopped in the courtyards,
the troops have left town, their escape route
long since publicised, along with the catechism:
even the gods have their messages from above.
The lottery numbers have fallen, been forgotten
and still this chatter of fortune. A finger rests
on a ring finger, the roughness of the knuckle
tests the surety of ceremonies; brides, cars
of ancient model, rice thrown then falling
from couples. The promise from all of us
to uphold what is right and true—
until it fails us. And then the promise to be held.
All the flags folded and placed in their lockers,
the teenagers sweating in gymnasiums,
lucky escapees from the war on childhood.
The winner of another contest has been announced
who has never won something like this before.
The advertisement says so. Half moon, half naked
we lie around the pool. The day's newspapers
flat on their tables, their headlines rest assured.
The wind picks up and steals their news
and palm trees wave an apology. The water,
so much colder this year. The road sign says
Another Kilometre and all the others recoil. Fortune,
wearing its badge, favours the brave and more often
the foolish, but still misses its autocue. A saw
cuts open another fresh tree and doesn't count
the year rings. The hooded marsupial leaves
droppings, calendar markings, on the stump:
I must get up today, find another forest, listen
to the sea again, its hushing shushing
of a noisy planet to sleep, to war, then further relaxation.

A Series of Good Investments

He sits with his thumbs in knots
a sparrow nestled in his stomach rolls
no need now for further talk of flight
or the lack therof, no need for further, distance
or any departure time, long distance call or marker.
No need for further talk.

—

Waking early, he returns to sleep.

—

Every childhood memory now tries
to overwhelm him, laugh and carry him
into their tombs. He stands at the entrance
to each, evades their attacks
then pushes them into the silence.

—

He sits beside a river and without moving
or disrobing dives in naked. He hears
the melodies of fish, looks up
lipreads the love calls of birds he cannot name
and can no longer find a reason to.

—

A whiphand, without its whip.

—

The desperate need for things to finish
has been arrested outside the city gates.
The trial begins tomorrow and, it is said,
no result is expected

—

There was consciousness, unconsciousness, preconsciousness,
a conscious effort, an unconscious action, a preconscious knowing,
a conscious reminder, an unconscious thought, a preconcious doubt.
They walked together along the riverbank, wondering why
they'd never enjoyed each others company before.

—

Several of us will be visiting
several others of us later.
You're welcome to come. He,
of course, will be there, his sparrow
stretched across his shoulder blades
a motorcade running down his back
and, when he looks down, something
remarkably like a city
but nothing like a building
will come into view on his chest.

—

The city lifts its ban on autumn.
Maintenance crews lean on their shovels.

Prayer

I am breathing my eyes open,
air leaves me, a mist of words.
I am speaking to the breathing
air. And what the air's missing
I speak. There is no answer
to my breathing, but I hear
the flutter of a bird's wing,
the curl of a cloud through air.
This is as close as I come.

Bedroom Psalm

I find that I'm on my knees and the rest of me
forms in a body shape around them. My knees
can't feel or at least don't want to. If there were witnesses
they'd see a man on his knees, head bowed,
eyes about to close in a darkened bedroom,
not a torn-clothed man, bleeding in the desert.
Wherever that wounded man kneels, he waits (why?)
for hands connected to a whisper to tend him,
a soothing hush to sweep across his bones,
surfspray for miles of dead grass.

I am on my knees, but carpet won't touch them
and neither will the sands on which I scrape my question mark.
I want fingertips, any will do, to pitter-patter on my skin,
take a grip on the crystal glass that holds my blood.

O you without ears –
Hear me
You without eyes –
Look, this shape's alive!
You with nothing but everything –
What do you want from me?

On my knees, for one reason or another, all day
or all my life. I can't remember when my soul
dropped through the shopping bag, but I'm sure
the cleaning staff were well prepared, even allowed
to keep a little for themselves. My hands on my knees.
My head bent to the sandy carpet and the word
on my lips, whatever it is, will do.

Screen Print Activist

Hi. I'm Che Guevara.
You know me. I'm on all those t-shirts.
Sort of stringy black hair
and a beret arrangement.
You can buy me at bong shops
or any good protest stall.

Someone said the other day
I look like Jon English,
'Hollywood Seven' era.
That surprised me:
I don't speak English.

Another bloke who had me on
(sweaty fella, don't know if he showers)
thought I played better guitar
than Hendrix. His mate said,
Nah, Guevara's a rhythm guitarist.
He thought 'Redemption Song'
was my best. That I'd gone
to live with Haile Selasie,
the spiritual king of Cuba.

A girl in America was asked
why she was wearing Saddam.
She laughed – so they
threw her in prison. And I thought
I'd died for nothing . . .

Character Actor

It's difficult sitting with you,
sipping a coffee. The thing can't be done
with any spontaneity. Who knows
when the movie cameras will arrive.

These are not the candid kind,
or camcorder, they're cinematic,
rolled along and flanked
by men with megaphones.

So it's difficult.
A cigarette held between fingers
lets rise my way of being
ready for discovery.

When I flick my hair,
move my cigarette pack,
you'll want to look at me.
Don't! Just gaze over my shoulder.

They could be here
any second. Shhh, watch me
blow my smoke around.

Gone Wonderland

Boats sail into the harbour with masts at half-mast.
Black suits megaphone, *Stop crying, it's not every day
there's an execution of power.* Someone shouts, *I have a dream*
and someone shouts louder, *Over my dead body!*
Ghost towns everywhere, but the economy booms
so loud we put fingers shaped like guns in our ears.
(Statistics bear this out and cover up the rest)
A sensible range of opinion is offered the opportunity
to strut the catwalk, but keeps walking past windows
wet with a soapy star's tears. The Opera House joins
the boats on the harbour, floats, looks at its watch:
it's going to be a long day's sailing and an even longer
sell-off. The black suits change to plain clothes,
set their weapons to seek the distraught.

Eclipse

It becomes when it takes
air from your lungs and is more
when you try to breathe again. It has no shape
but yours. And even that is borrowed. Do you have
time for the forest and the tiny mouse that hides there?
The children playing outside on the lawn
would like to know: how can a black skipping rope
in the hands of a little girl be anything but an omen?
All right, if you say it's not. But light is coming
from a moon you cannot see. Or refuse to. Or once saw
and forgot, flung back to a planet spinning on its great I
that can never be true. But would sometimes like to be.

You Say You Want a Revolution, Well . . .

Our feather-thin gloves, laid gently on a coffee table,
        beneath a lamp that offers, in turn, lamplight
or shadow, but always the outline of an unlit candle.

        And then there's the darkness.
        Finally.

Tune in your voice to the radio.

That is not static.

        I can hear the sun.
Burn, burn, there are millions of years
and a fat glob of planet stuck in our eyes.

Leave your shoes at the door. Leave the door, too.
Here you are, sit down, window-seat.
We've video-taped the "revolutionaries'" departure.
Raise your glass to the last of them
        disappearing over the horizon in sturdy trousers.

        Never whisper their names again,
even in jest (I'm serious), even when
        you're asked for a joke
in the hotels, skyscrapers and parliaments they built.

Those aren't fields burning,

it's that noisy sun again (a laugh-a-minute) turning red roofs
        to blue flames,
                hot investments

sign here_____ .

All the News

The latest film about a filmmaker makes its debut.
Many men are killed for the many killed
and we're told, while the killing goes on,
that whatever we want is at the touch of a button
but nobody uses buttons anymore.

Cities ban autumn. A maintenance issue.
Other seasons said to be nervous.
Older insecurities rise, all the paperwork
is complete and someone, somewhere
still believes enough in clocks
to tick off the appropriate boxes.

American Might

Because I can. And there's nothing else to do.
Well, there's the corn to harvest. And Mary Lou's
graduation, web-cammed and cable networked.
And what about that long lonely coyote call
calling me skyward from the bucket seat of my tractor?

She might, too. She's got a new banjo,
a plane ticket's chewed-up stub
and a brand new view
beneath a spinning hubcap
on a bombed out road.

We both might. So might many others.
The web poll says 95 percent and climbing,
the budget is expanding, the pipelines
are bursting, the underwater cables
pump live footage to the world.

We *might*.   No, we probably will.
Because history is a sore loser, fighter jets
have pet names, God is a proud, proud father
and our movies are aircraft hangers
for favourite flying dreams.

ID

Flowers, not supposed to be here in winter,
not supposed to be singing.

A raft of changes. Then a life raft of changes.

From over the horizon, the obligatory.

Hippies have left their hippy masks all over
the forest floor. A lost child tries one on.

An American flag, wrapped in an American flag.

The bouquet of wilted flowers
after their friends' torch song.
Life raft without life or water.

The moment has passed. There'll be another.
But not right now.

Deny every compulsion until we know its intention.
We must.

What child is lost? Does he not have himself,
his hippy mask?

An American flag, lining the insides of all coffins.

And flowers.

He Will Become a Musician

There is always a scene on a beach,
where all last words are spoken. A father,
a son – a husband and whoever. A wife,
a forgotten towel, twirling gulls.

Whenever there is not a moment on a beach
there is a cemetery. Gravestones waiting
for new last words. When the beach
and the cemetery are one, there is an aerial view

of a windswept coastal scene. The moan
of uillean pipes or cellos. Perhaps a chorus
of a soon-to-be pop song, something
dull for the hum of bruises. The view

through guitar-string branches
is a stage of life. A wave sung shore,
fistfuls of seaweed dragged through the undertow.

Convincing Ground

The site, in the Victorian town of Portland, of the first recorded
massacre of Aborigines by white Australians.

We drive past cemetries,
headstones bend in coastal breeze.
All afternoon we drive, and headstones
give no shadow. We wind up our windows,
clouds retreat, we pretend the day is blue.
We drive past paddocks, scar trees
hold orders of service. We drive past towns
full of cemeteries, broken pub verandas.
We drive past cemeteries: wheat crops, wind farms,
the unused olive branches. We drive past
pools and lakes, pretend again the day is blue.
Headstones rise all round us, we see them
walk to courts of law. We drive and drive
and drive, in search of an open grave.

Even the Elect

Spotlight beam catches
the light of the world.
It takes on that usual
human form,
points to scars
for authenticity,
evades the beam, finds itself,
again, led to the desert.
There, spotlight shine
shows me wrestling
space where a body should be.

Refurbishment

A choir, somewhere, finishes.
Marble silence.
Fragments of stained glass window
in the unconfirmed
rumours of wheat;
a puzzle
for the girl in a black dress,
her hands white and offered
to a Cubist sky.
A headstone kite forgets its place:
an appendix to *History*, not the Title Page.
The darkened door further darkened,
the spire has no bells, the roof's removed,
and saints are stars. The crucifix
replaced by a mirror.

Essay after Interest

after Les Murray

I have no further interest in love, that goes without saying, it's been said before but, yes, I've said it again. Neither do I have any interest in sex, God, faith, truth, lies, honesty, death, hope, pessimism, happiness or despair. That doesn't leave much, you say, but I beg to differentiate: people – male, female, children – animals, plants, sky, heaven, hell, dancing, walking, swimming, flying, breathing or holding my breath. *Why don't you just* . . . well, because I have no interest in suicide, saving lives, being alive or not, buzzing or feeling numb. I have no interest in meditation, contemplation, yoga, prayer, Pilates, religion – Eastern, Western, forgotten or recently revived – food, drink, family, writing (especially irony), singing, painting, collaging, mixing, cooking, hurting, healing, touching, smelling, tasting, hearing, no interest, none at all. That doesn't mean I'm interested in disinterest, being uninteresting or boring; I have no interest in these or philosophies, theories, contingencies, policies, possibilities, marriage, divorce, separation, relation, loneliness or friends, smiling or crying, laughing, throwing up, filling my gut, staying put or moving house, travelling or standing still. I'm not interested in money, poverty, riches, theft or holding on, nor am I interested in difference, similarity, changing sides or playing fair, my job, a new start, a fresh face, an old trick, a new dog, dreams, responsibilities, tickling, feathers, skin or teeth. I am no longer interested and if it wasn't for my forensic interest in my loss of interest in all the things I'm not interested in, I'd be ready, finally, to be known as I am.

Lining Up Time

the queue leads to the stadium. which is death, heaven, hell, or a
stadium.
from our vantage point above, those in the queue seem static. but move

into the queue and we're walking forwards. those in front are no
longer there.
neither is the stadium. those behind stretch further away. yet we're
in a gathering.

we think we're moving forward, but there's no stadium. we may not be
at all.
back at our vantage point, the stadium's below. there may be other
stadiums,

other queues, but how can they concern us? we have this queue
its stadium that surely no one is entering. but people line up.

White Fluffy Clouds, Angels Playing Harps

The worst part is I believed
I once knew something,
that standing featureless
in white porcelain
I could name all the parts of my soul
and everyone's.

But now, aware that I am
only a reflection in white porcelain,
I know the worst part:
my body is a window that opens
onto a wall and I look out,
name all the parts of the brickwork.

With everyone else, I hope
there's another side, where windows
are unnecessary, and all the souls'
parts name their bodies,
those features in white porcelain.

Everyone there with me named
by their worst parts, opening walls
onto windows reflected on porcelain,
pretending to believe they know something,
naming themselves apart from their bodies.

Ode to a Frying Christ

Christmas has come early again,
like last year,
and there's not enough time
now or ever after
for sleep, magic, prayer,
or strolling hand-in-hand near the ocean,
toes touching water
soft enough for walking on.

Trapped in the crowd,
I hold my cup of beans
wait for a miracle of loaves, wine,
or Christmas tree leaves, falling like scales
on to fish you're still frying on a beach
two thousand years ago.

Sharing the Lion's Share

i am afraid of dying   in a house with white lace curtains. afraid
someone will take me from where I'm convalescing   usher me into a
brick veneer house with no trees or plants beside it and someone will
cook me a bowl of porridge and leave it steaming on the bedside table
while i look through white lace curtains at the house across the street
with white lace curtains and no trees or plants and one white lion with
a spout of water rising from a smiling mouth.

there'll be no other food so i'm worried i'll chew the porridge with lips
pressed together   concerned the smell coming down the corridor is sheep
brain frying for dinner. i will look across and find the porridge bowl
replaced by a hot dry crumpet. when its steam has risen i'll begin to give
up worrying about the smell of brains and accept these things have come
to me and death and some things like these will come to everyone.

i close my eyes and step through wet crumpet to the sound of bubbling
porridge   the smell of linen sheets flapping round my eyes   and a
white-faced lion in purple robes saying well done   you made it through
let's stand together spout water from our mouths forever maybe reach
the nature strip if we catch the breeze   wait   hold your pose
i'll open the door a little wider

Angle

after John Forbes

Absolutely serious about everything.
And that's only the beginning of the problem,
only one way of blinking a flutter free of its horse,
returning to a stable where the best miracles
are cast-off as miraculous receptions.
You can only pick them up if you tilt your head
in the direction of all that mean-faced charity.
A flutter is also a bet. I'll wager it's useless to remind
all the angles in heaven that a perfect circle is so
because its wings have been clipped.

Demographic Manifesto
for David Prater

embryo – 12 years

You will look out from behind steel fences when you are, a) dwelling in your nation of origin; or, b) applying for the sun to shine on you from a different direction. Subset "a" will be permitted to leave at 6.00 pm.

12 – 30

You will be responsible for making hamburgers and/or increasing the gross in the national or multinational product. You will purchase coloured sunglasses and (while grossing fast foods or other products) you will flip them onto your forehead. You will set your sights lower for the weekend when you will fry your brains on designer genes.

30 – 50

You will key a set of numbers of your choice into the company of your choice, chosen from a closed list of companies owned by subsets of companies in the list who will also provide the aforementioned numbers. You will not be required to make hamburgers, but you will be responsible for making the requirement for hamburgers and/or coloured sunglasses.

Alternatively, you can choose to be alternative. You'll be permitted to enjoy the nation's gross products, but will be also allowed to wonder whether you are. This will fry your brain – despite designer genes.

50 – 70

You will tow caravans at slow speeds on all available roads. You must not apply for a number beyond the numbers you have accumulated during 30 – 50. Any hats thrown into the ring must be left to collect dust until after 6.00 pm. You must be seen only in warm climates wearing large shorts.

70 +

You must lie in bed and press red buttons if still alive. If not, the pressing will be conducted on your behalf. Your need for assistance with breathing and other rudimentary tasks will place strain on the gross nationals, however, they must accept you as a product. Take any complaints the gross nationals make about your alleged non-production to the alternatives. You will look out from behind brick fences while only the finest quality clouds drift past your view. Speaking will not be permitted, however, grunting will be optional.

Insight

Feel the bones in ya nose.
Not that hard bit the bridge,
the bit below ya nostrils.
Feel round there, feel the bones
crinkle in ya fingers. They're the ones
you'll smash with an uppercut.

But that's not enough:
you gotta keep the punch
goin up til ya push
the bastard's nose into his brain.
That's how ya kill a man,
that's hand-to-hand.

Ya can take ya fingers
outta ya nose now.
Filthy habit, don't do that.
Do ya know what I'm talking about?
You gotta listen to me lad.
Give me a look at ya knuckles.

Father's Club

On a backyard table
we place stubbies on the edges,
then hug them to the middle.
Ninepins for mechanical arms.

We have brought our meat,
children and dreams. Randomly
we laugh at all three.

On a hyper green lawn,
kids listen in black and white:
'Laughter is Happy'
'Daddies cook Barbies'
'Summer is Forever'

In who-got-the-first-wicket-chatter,
meat smell rises from the hotplate,
untended. In family units,
chops, sausages and hamburgers
slow sizzle to charcoal.

When winter comes we'll wish again
to sit here, ignoring the lines
on each other's faces. Today,
we hold stubbies in our laps like skulls.

My Wheelie Bin's Big Day

Full of everything I can offer her, she will go to her groom
tomorrow, his bad breath and roaring. But I will walk her
proudly to her nuptials, her lid closed, no more of my leftover
life to swallow. She reaches the nature strip and stars
hold their breath. Paper pile haggard on one side,
recycle bucket on the other, these attendants look up
to her: she's patient and full with the promise of this
and every Wednesday night. But, O, the hollow promise.

The recycle bucket tumbles, the papers are delivered
to where news is of no consequence. Again this morning
her groom lifted her to suburban heights and she went,
lid over wheels to him, offered him everything.
But it wasn't enough. It is never enough. He left her
for another, then another, and another. She stands
where he dropped her. Open-mouthed, surprised again
by her emptiness. I wheel her back into my life.

Baggage

You don't need to see a suitcase on the veranda
to know a suitcase is there. It's on the veranda
no matter how hard it tries to be in the cupboard.

Empty coat hangers console each other
with the memory of clothes. The suitcase
is closed, but who needs to be told what's inside?

The suitcase will go where it must,
conveyor belts will turn and bus wheels spin;
the suitcase will allow it.

No one needs to see
a veranda without a suitcase
to know where the suitcase has gone.

Faultlines

See how over is the sunset, how rotten is the pear. See how open
is the fridge door, how empty is your lounge. See how happy
were the children, how timeless is the clock, how forgotten are your vows.
See how still the crowd is and how shrill the whistle sounds. See how
filmic is your vision, but how far you are from screens. See how blonde
the model's hair is and how dull the sun seems. See the ore shards
jump for magnets, hear the shaking of the tree. See the air form holes
for fruit fall, see how rotten is the pair. See how groundless is the earth,
how forgotten is the eulogy and how travelled is the path. See far distant
are the crossroads, hear the wind blow through the bones there.

Better Late Than, etc.

for Simone

There is a quality that only the music of the past possesses:
a bright guitar in the night sky, played slide; a grandmother's voice
as she points out the window of a family wagon, something
beautiful we turned to see but missed. That music is playing now
and we reach for the volume dial, an eyeball floating in its tear.

There is a quality the past has that makes it sound like memory,
yet holds us here, present tense. We doubt the sun could share
our faith in daylight and when we turn it over in our minds
we know that the night has always asked us a question we've failed to answer.

Music itself has a quality that only memory possesses. The past
plays itself in even the newest radio tunes and we wish
for lives without mistakes. We laugh at the echo our voices make,
our laughter joining the notes of a song we'll never remember,
the everyday music of the past, the days without each other.

Required

Caring Individual (Full Time, Class 1)
for Give a Shit International

Due to global demand, Give a Shit International has recently opened an arm in Australia. Our head office, located from street to beach to workplace to public park, requires another Caring Individual to join our failing business.

You will have a complete lack of customer focus with highly developed communication skills, but most likely utterly hopeless organisational and time management skills. You will enjoy liaising with a wide range of people – who may not enjoy liaising with you – and you will have no technological skills whatsoever.

Caring Individuals at Give a Shit International require some critical skills. You will have a proven capacity to ignore deadlines and you will not only work well in a team, you will *only* be able to work in a team. You will have no understanding of budget imperatives and will be experienced in ensuring projects blow out their stated financial parameters. You will be a hopeless self-starter and completely inflexible when it comes to those who say *Why do you bother giving a shit?*

Salary: Pro-Rata absolutely nothing (Class 1), without superannuation contributions or any salary packaging options, staff development or training opportunities. This position commences as soon as possible and will not end until you die – with the possibility of an extension beyond this initial contract.

ID

i

Before an eye meets his eye,
mirror is surf, he waves and waves
crashing into the shore.

ii

The teenager shouts –
I will die in front of my mirror! I will
outstare myself!

He jumps,
the mirror pulls away,
but catches him

between glass and wall.
He spits limestone, blames
God and Narcissus and
whoever else will listen.

My soul is itself
seen and gone!

iii

The ceiling holds her breasts,
she says. He doesn't bother to look.

iv

In the mirror, the orchestra
practises waving to the conductor
– he falls into the glass,

applause dies down,
horses ride through spray
and the music of a house on fire.

v

Only bones and blood,
obeying gravity.

vi

His semen dripping from her,
she wipes with a tissue,
he looks up at his face;
red at the cheeks, white at the lips,
wipes.

vii

At the family dinner table,
the teenager stares at his reflection
in the butter-knife blade.

Practice

i play.   drums.
I mean, i don't   really
play drums. I mean
it's hard   you know
the rhythm. therhythm's   hard. I get
my feet wrong. and the sticks.
In my hands.   wrong, I get the wrong
drum.   I mean, I hit the right drum
        with the wrong   stick.
I like   drums. it's
        hard, though. to prac
tise. no one likes   drums.
        Thenoise.   n
my rhythm.   I play. drum   s.

Dear Kids

for Hannah and Hugo

It's just so fantastic
that you're alive.
You can live all you want.
You can be something.
Or nothing at all.
You can do both and then
decide to be neither.
You'll be happy. Then sad.
Then happy again. You'll hear
The Police sing, 'Walking
on the Moon' while you're
walking on the moon.
Dumb people will say
they're smart
and you'll know it.
No one will ever jump on your guitar.
If they do, play piano
right back at them. Don't listen
to me! Then listen closely.
Have a bite to eat.
Fly away. Then come back.
I'll be waiting in my wings
with my heart outstretched.

You're Lying Again

This is how I learnt to lie:
first sit down then stretch back.
See, I'm at it again.
But let me tell you about
when I learnt to lie
with a girl. She said
it would ruin everything.
And though she did it,
she wasn't lying. She said
there was no pain,
but I remember tears.
She'd say I'm lying again,
that I remember other things.
So, instead, I'll tell you about
my first lie. I was lying down
getting undressed by mum.
She tore off my pants
and the toy car fell
from my three-year-old pocket:
Q. Where did you get this?
A. It fell in there.
I held mum's hand,
stood small at the counter
said Sorry Shopkeeper.
I'm not lying now,
that's the face-covered truth about lies.

How Many Light Bulbs Does it Take

Touch me, here, on the cheek. I am not a strong man.
My bones are bubbles and my hairs are needles
and I run when I should walk. Put your many fingers
through my hair. Lie me down and talk to me
but please don't speak. Stroke my fingernails
with your skin, whisper my name with your hair
then do it again. I am patient. Write me a letter
while I watch you, sign my name on it, then argue
about the cost of not living. I have waited. And I am.
Here. Touch. My heart has lion's claws but doesn't roar.
Hover over me, a human light bulb buzzing.

The Bedroom Clock

Children need clocks in their bedrooms
that ring when childhood is over,
    when it's time to run
    to a river of buildings,
        pulling suits from out of their lunchbags.

How young are you, said the child to the willow
that guards a river of tiaras. I am as young as the minute-
hand on the clock I'm drawing upon your wall.

I put my arm around her. I love you Dad, she says.
I love you, too, I say. And hold just a little bit back.

Children need to know when bedroom stories
    are bedroom games,
    when their mothers' arms around them
    are holding onto their husbands.

How old are you, said the mother to the son
who hid his pubic hair. I'm as old as the backyard gum
that's lost all its leaves. Please don't ask me again.

I stroke her head, she smiles. Any tick of the clock
she will stare up from the bed on which she curls
and see that I'm a man. But not this minute or year.

Children need a letter to explain
they are no longer children, clouds
have their own shapes and love
is a warm nail through your lungs

How old are you, said the bedroom clock
to the sleeping man. I am as old as his dreams
replied the child awake in the corner.

The Persistent Myth

a real time update

The room has no furniture.
He looks out the floor
to ceiling window
at the dark and the sea.
He hears the snapping
of wind at an empty flagpole
chains around its ankle.

This side of the miracle
of disembodiment
his body looks fit
if thin and naked.
The woman next to him
wishes she wasn't. He has
no time but he wastes it
feels his hands disappear
into her dissolving breasts.

She kisses him awake
then slaps his face. *Stop it, mother,*
he says, *I have no need for your womb here.*
He is his own. She hiccups,
he furnishes the room by memory.

Love Song for St Simeon

It is a pleasure to be held in the arms of a fool
whose fingers have whittled down to ice cubes,
whose breath belongs to a horse in the mist
of myth, riddles – ideas asleep in language.

You threw your faded red-green pointy hat
to the ground for the weary street sweeper
to pick up and lay upon his back. It's the cross
he'll carry to the priest who stole his song.

Your arms are laden with fruit; our pink shapes
pulled from the garden after that morning walk;
the pulse of summer on our necks, a pierced side
already bleeding. What we have is the reminder

of that winter when the chalet slid down
the hillside to become the town's clock tower;
the hearth that gave its twigs, the hands
that ticked beneath a bear's head rug in flame.

We have our memories for locking away where
no one bothers to speak of keys or all the water
used to make them. A triple six fits the lock
on any dice that's rolled before the King

who was, of course, flown in from a city far away
where no one lives, always a thrown leash from here.
Let the little children and other children
come into the castle, dragging dead dogs behind them.

Review

There are canyons where my eyes were,
the shadows of birds float over them.

Where my mind was, I can still smell
bouquets from your last performance.

The heart has isolation chambers
holding every person we have held,

but there are no windows. Our souls
are hills invaded by suburbs. I watch

mending the roof of my rain-damaged
mouth. After the storm, the canyons

opening wider. I look into the absence
of your eyes, ticket stubs swirl in the wind.

Aftermath

Trying to believe my own rhetoric, trying
not to announce myself
in the second person. Imagining a baby
emerging from something other
than a womb. And then scratching, scratching
her head at the image and my Oh So Clever
playfulness. The inevitable line about wondering
if anyone is listening. And then the yawn
as all of us recognise that every line was, of course,
for all of us afterall. Cleverly in sync
we do the dishes in separate houses.

Awake, Despite the Hour

after Kevin Hart

Please come to me. I know the universe
is falling apart, but please come, regardless of the holes
in every leaf through which the rain is falling. Come to me
despite the mistakes I've made, in fact, because of them.
Please come, despite the hunger grinding bellies I cannot see,
the lives I'll never change; come to me though they need you more.
Come though I see you, a lump behind the curtain
of friends' and lovers' eyes: they turn from me,
they know the world is what their eyes fall upon,
but you see where vision ends, touch where bodies are not.
Please come to me and do not leave, hold me, despite the homeless,
lonely, loveless who call your name with every word.
Come to me, sit with me, tell me not to worry,
birds have nests, or say something about the sky,
that storm clouds are useless without their rain
and leaves with holes have smiles. Please come to me,
here, now, take me to this place I am and cannot go alone.